Contemporary Musicians
AND THEIR MUSIC™

Fall Out Boy

Sarah Sawyer

ROSEN
PUBLISHING
New York

Published in 2009 by The Rosen Publishing Group, Inc.
29 East 21st Street, New York, NY 10010

Library of Congress Cataloging-in-Publication Data

Sawyer, Sarah.
Fall Out Boy / Sarah Sawyer.—1st ed.
    p. cm.—(Contemporary musicians and their music)
Includes bibliographical references.
ISBN-13: 978-1-4042-1819-2 (library binding)
ISBN-13: 978-1-4358-5127-6 (pbk)
ISBN-13: 978-1-4042-7872-1 (6 pack)
1. Fall Out Boy (Musical group)—Juvenile literature. 2. Rock musicians—United States—Biography—Juvenile literature. I. Title.
ML3930.F25S38 2008
782.42166092'2—dc22
[B]

2008006922

Manufactured in Malaysia

On the cover: Pictured here are the four members of the band Fall Out Boy.

Contents

Introduction

Since coming onto the scene in 2001, Fall Out Boy has earned itself an enthusiastic legion of fans. The band, of course, counts this as a blessing—although, as singer Pete Wentz explained to VH1.com, some fans have an odd way of expressing their appreciation. "Someone gave me an envelope of razor blades with what appeared to be blood on them not long ago. I'm not sure I understood the sentiment, even when they said it was just nail polish. And someone heard I like yellow flowers, so every day I get, like, eighty million daisies."

Fall Out Boy's frontman, Pete Wentz, plays his bass at the House of Blues.

Sounds freaky, but don't worry. Most fans show their admiration in a more conventional way—by buying their albums and helping them win awards. In 2006, for example, Fall Out Boy won Teen Choice Awards in three categories: Rock Track for "Dance, Dance"; Single for "Dance, Dance"; and Rock Group. They also won the Viewer's Choice award at the MTV Video Music Awards. Then, in 2007, they did it again, winning Teen Choice Awards in the Single and Rock Group categories and earning the coveted Best Group award at the MTV Music Awards.

And when their fans buy albums, they really buy albums. Fall Out Boy's 2005 release, *From Under the Cork Tree*, debuted at number 9 on the Billboard 200 albums chart and sold more than 68,000 copies the first week it was out. As the weeks passed and word spread, the album eventually sold more than 2.5 million copies in the United States, going double platinum. Their second album did even better. In its first week, *Infinity on High* hit number 1 on the Billboard 200 and sold 260,000 copies.

One thing's for sure. Fans' emotions run high for this emo band, which translates into huge gigs for the group. In 2005, they joined the Nintendo Fusion Tour and played with groups like the Starting Line, Motion City Soundtrack, Boys Night Out, and Panic! at the Disco. And their gigs are getting bigger every day.

Subsequently, they headlined the Young Wild Things Tour (which featured Gym Class Heroes, Plain White T's, and Cute Is What We Aim For) and kicked off with a sold-out show in Columbus, Ohio.

Fall Out Boy has certainly hit some bumps in the road. It hasn't been all rainbows and unicorns for the band. But all in all, they've enjoyed growing success, and their fans—maybe fans like you?—just can't get enough of them.

Chapter One

Meet the Band

In 2001, friends Pete Wentz and Joe Trohman started playing in indie bands in the Chicago metropolitan area (sometimes called Chicagoland). They both listened to a lot of Green Day, the Descendents, and 1980s emo pioneers the Smiths. One day, while shopping in a Borders bookstore, Trohman overheard a guy talking about the band Neurosis. He liked the band, too, so he introduced himself. That's how Patrick Stump met the other two and joined the band. The three of them needed two more players to flesh out their act, so they recruited T. J. Raccine to play guitar and a musician simply credited as "Mike" to play drums. These were the members of the band when they recorded their mini-LP, *Fall Out Boy's Evening Out with Your Girlfriend*, in 2002.

It wasn't long before Raccine and "Mike" left and Andy Hurley showed up to play guitar. The band we now know as Fall Out Boy was born and started playing fairly regular gigs at the Knights of Columbus Hall in Arlington, Illinois. You know the place if you've seen the video for Fall Out Boy's "Dead on Arrival." It was filmed there.

Rumor has it that the band played its first two gigs without a name. Then, at the end of one gig, they asked the audience for name suggestions and someone yelled "Fall Out Boy!" An obscure reference to a character from the animated television program *The Simpsons*, Fallout Boy is the sidekick to Radioactive Man, one of Bart Simpson's favorite comic book characters. The name stuck, and they've used it ever since.

That, briefly, is how the group got together. Now let's meet the members one at a time.

Pete Wentz

Born Peter Lewis Kingston Wentz III on June 5, 1979, Wentz is the bassist, back-up vocalist, and lyricist for Fall Out Boy. He's often told reporters that his first memory is of listening to "Build Me Up Buttercup" by the Foundations while in the car with his dad.

Pete Wentz at Cameo, a nightclub in Miami Beach, Florida.

As a student at Chicagoland's New Trier Township High School and North Shore Country Day School, he was an avid soccer player. He graduated from high school in 1997 and went to DePaul University to study political science; he remains one semester short of graduation.

Maybe it was political science (and seeing politicians cultivate connections) that taught him how to network. Maybe he was just born with it. But there's no doubt his celebrity is amplified by the many blog entries, interviews, and other publicity materials he sends out into cyberspace. And Fall Out Boy's rise in popularity has given him ample opportunity to make connections and explore his creativity. In addition to his music career, Wentz's other business ventures include: Clandestine Industries, a company that distributes clothing, books, and other items; Decaydance Records, an imprint of Fueled by Ramen productions, which has signed bands including Panic! At the Disco, Sweet Blood Stacy, and others; a film production company called Bartskull Films; and a nightclub called Angels & Kings. He's a busy guy for sure, and everything he touches seems to turn to gold—at least in his professional life.

Wentz's personal life—as with many high-energy, creative people—has seen its highs and lows. One of the lowest lows

YOU KNOW YOU'RE A STAR WHEN THEY NAME A BASS AFTER YOU

In acknowledgement of Pete Wentz's influence on the next generation of bass players, the musical instrument company Fender created the Fender Squier Pete Wentz Precision Bass guitar. The company describes the bass as follows: "Decorated with Pete's own red bat/ heart design on the body and a black bat/diamond fingerboard inlay at the 12th fret, a 9.5"-radius C-shaped maple Jazz Bass neck with a rolled-edge laminated maple fingerboard, a thunderous Duncan Designed™ PB-105 split single-coil pickup, chrome hardware, and an eye-catching, three-ply, red shell pickguard, Squier calls this special design, 'A darkly beautiful bass that'll rock your face off . . .'" Looks like they might be right!

came in 2005, when he was hospitalized after taking an overdose of an anti-anxiety medication called Ativan. "I was isolating myself further and further," he recalled to *Spin* magazine, "and the more I isolated myself, the more isolated I'd feel. I wasn't sleeping. I just wanted my head to shut off, like, I just wanted to completely stop thinking about anything at all."

His solution at the time was to take too many pills, but he's finding healthier ways to cope with stress now. One way he found to keep himself steady was to lean on his family for emotional support, which is why he decided to move back home and live with his parents for a while. It wasn't too long before he felt stronger and more stable and moved into a place in Los Angeles nearer the rest of the band. Accepting help and support when he needed it seems to have really paid off.

Another low was the time someone stole revealing pictures Wentz had taken of himself and posted them all over the

MORE ABOUT SUICIDE

If you or someone you love feels suicidal, there is help. Call 1-800-SUICIDE (784-2433) or visit http://www.suicide.org for resources, information, and support.

Internet. But he handled the situation with a strong sense of self and knowledge of his own priorities. "It's been a tough couple of weeks for me lately," he posted on his Web site shortly after the incident. "The only good thing about times of adversity is that you realize who your real friends and fans are—and the rest go away—which in my mind is an OK thing . . . After feeling badly about this for about 24 hours, I am now ready to get back to laughing."

One of the things many find most endearing about Wentz is how comfortable he appears to be with himself—especially regarding issues that give so many young people pause. Take, for example, the ease with which he discusses his bisexual tendencies. In interviews with *Blender* and *The Advocate*, he talked about times in his life when he's been attracted to—and even kissed—other men. He's honest about who he is, and that makes it easy for fans to relate to him, whether they are comfortable with his choices or not.

Of course, due to his celebrity, it's easy for things to snowball quickly. What started as a simple admission that he sometimes finds men attractive was magnified by the media until the general perception was that he was bisexual or gay. This was not his original intent. In an interview with *Rolling Stone*, Wentz clarified the issue. "I would never come out and say I'm gay," he explained, "because I'm not gay. There's part of me that kind of wishes I was gay, and I think that comes from anybody constantly wishing they were in the minority and constantly wants to be fighting everybody off."

This fluid identity, openness, and willingness to experiment is part of his charm. He doesn't take himself too seriously. He's the punkish boy next door—and that's why he's so well-loved.

Joe Trohman

Joseph Trohman was born September 1, 1984. He was raised

in South Russell, just east of Cleveland, Ohio, and moved to Chicagoland when he was about twelve. He attended Washburne Junior High and New Trier

With his curly hair, shaggy beard, and playful attitude, Joe Trohman is sometimes seen as the band's jokester. Trohmaniacs love his signature jump and spin.

Township High School in Winnetka, Illinois, which is where he met Wentz.

Trohman sometimes goes by the name JoeTro. Another of his nicknames is Trohmania, which he got because of his signature spin. You may have seen it in the "This Ain't a Scene, It's an Arms Race" video. He does it and knocks a bottle over. Once, when spinning like that, he hit Wentz in the face, causing him to get stitches. The nickname stuck after that. Joe's fans sometimes refer to themselves as Trohmaniacs.

Though Wentz and Trohman have been friends forever, they have very different styles. Where Wentz is a little edgier socially, Trohman comes off as a bit more conventional. One of his early memories is discovering the *Star Wars* trilogy. "I still collect tons

COMBUSTIBLE COIFFURES

Q: What do Michael Jackson and Joe Trohman have in common?

A: They've both learned the hard way to keep their curly hair away from theater pyrotechnics.

In December 2007, Joe's 'fro went up in flames while performing at the Jingle Ball. He's OK and he finished the song, but he may never finish getting teased about it by his band mates.

of action figures," he said in an interview with StarWars.com. "My closet in my apartment is full—95 percent of *Star Wars* toys. . . . I'm also looking to get my hands on some A material original action figures from the '70s."

He loves video games, too, and eagerly discusses all the finer points of them in interviews. It's Trohman's simple loves that allow people to relate to him. People feel like they know him— and in some ways, they do. He shares a lot of the interests and hobbies of the typical American guy. Their lives have a lot in common—with one exception. Trohman's a rock star.

Rock star status means he gets to do things that average guys don't. He's been on *Saturday Night Live*, *One Tree Hill*, and the *Late Show with David Letterman*. He's also performed in more concerts than we'd ever have room to list here. He's less extroverted than his band mate Wentz, but he's always up for fun in a "normal guy" way.

Patrick Stump

"I think you can totally be a totally normal kid from the suburbs of Chicago and go off and play shows," said Patrick Stump to DiamondbackOnline.com. "It's one of those things that when you go home, you're still the nerd you were when you left, and

Patrick Stump, the band's lead vocalist, can be shy with the press, but he shines onstage.

your parents still get to yell at you about cleaning up your room, and your girlfriend still drags you to the pet store." Such is a typical observation of Fall Out Boy's offbeat vocalist.

Patrick Martin Stumph was born on April 27, 1984, in Glenview, Illinois, which is in the greater Chicago area. He changed the spelling of his last name from Stumph to Stump when he joined Fall Out Boy so that people would have an easier time pronouncing it. While Wentz writes most of the lyrics for Fall Out Boy's songs, Stump writes—and sings—the music.

Before the band took off, Stump worked in not one, but two record stores. He's a real music fan, preferring to listen to music rather than getting caught up in the celebrity scene and tabloid gossip. He's quieter in some ways than some of his band mates. He doesn't like giving interviews or doing photo shoots, and he sometimes gets flustered when he makes public appearances. Once, at an early television appearance, he got so freaked out by being onstage that after his interview he went to shake Wentz's hand instead of the interviewer's. It wasn't a big deal, but it tells you something about him: he's sort of shy, and not entirely at home being front and center.

"I'm horribly uncomfortable with being the frontman. With Pete, I get to be the anti-frontman," he said, as quoted on TV.com. "There's no attention on me; I just get to sing."

In fact, Stump wasn't a singer before he joined Fall Out Boy. He joined thinking he'd be the drummer, but then the guitarist quit and he decided to teach himself guitar and voice. His fans are so glad he did. And, while he's shy about his personal life, he's sure not shy about his guitar playing or about music in general. He talks about music comfortably and with enthusiasm every chance he gets. His enthusiasm shows in some of the "signature moves" he's developed on guitar, including one he calls "the nerd in the basement" in which he holds the guitar over his head to play it.

Also—in case you're wondering—at five feet, four inches, he's the shortest member of Fall Out Boy. Yet he refuses to be self-consciousness about his height. "There's a song by Randy

Newman called 'Short People,' and I think it's hilarious," Stump said, as quoted on MovieTome.com. "I think it's perfect for me, because . . . the tag line is 'short people got no reason to live' right . . . and that's like, the main line of the song. So that's funny to say about yourself. 'Oh, I'm short man. Everything sucks' right . . . and to a certain degree I mock myself and I put myself down. But in all seriousness, I'm happy with myself and the song is totally in jest and the combination of the tone and lyrics is perfect for me. That's my song."

Andy Hurley

The newest member of Fall Out Boy, drummer Andrew John Hurley joined the band after its first album was released. He was born on May 31, 1980, in Milwaukee, Wisconsin. His father died when he was only five, and

Fall Out Boy's drummer, Andy Hurley, is certainly the most tattooed member of the band.

his mother, a nurse, raised him by herself. After his father passed away, he went through a rebellious phase that eventually gave way to the clean living he enjoys today.

"The rambunctious goof eventually became a pretty quiet and introspective kid, focused mostly on his music," one of his teachers told Drew Olson, senior editor of MilwaukeeOnline.com. "His circle of friends was pretty small, mostly just other kids who thought like he did and who also played music, mostly hard-core and punk type stuff. I still remember the band director at the time (Don Huenfeld), who has since retired, commenting on the fact that Andy was phenomenally talented and probably the best drummer he'd ever seen."

These days, Hurley is vegan, meaning that he doesn't eat meat, dairy, or any other animal-based foods. He is also into the "straight-edge" lifestyle, an alternative lifestyle and punk-music

FUN FACT

Hurley has 2,600 tattoos, each one a tiny square. He was nineteen when he got his first one, a large heart in the middle of his chest. He feels that his tattoos tell the story of his life like a diary would.

subculture that steers clear of all alcohol and drugs. Hurley's big high is playing the drums.

While he's played for many bands in the past, playing for one as big as Fall Out Boy has been an adjustment. "It's weird to see yourself on MTV or on a magazine somewhere," Hurley told OnMilwaukee.com, a Milwaukee newspaper. "It's an adjustment. But when that happens, I just look at it and say, 'I guess we're still out there.' We're not trying to do things in a specific way. We're still trying to push it and take chances."

Hurley's secret passion? Comic books! He reads and collects comics and is working on one of his own. Titled *Post Collapse*, it's about the end of the world—which he feels is not far off. "My whole thing is I'm not into civilization as a whole," he said, as quoted on TV.com. "The only actual solution is the eventual collapse and demise of civilization . . . I think it needs to happen, but I think no one, not even me, really wants it to happen."

Now that we've gotten to meet the band, in the next chapter we'll get to know the music a little better.

Chapter Two

The Music of Fall Out Boy

The first thing you're likely to notice about Fall Out Boy's songs is the length and wittiness of the titles. Generally, a song title is three words or less, but Fall Out Boy's song titles are often nearly a full sentence. Titles like "Our Lawyer Made Us Change the Name of this Song So We Wouldn't Get Sued" or "Champagne for My Real Friends, Real Pain for My Sham Friends" are simply much longer than the norm.

Many record label executives would think, "Oh, fans will never remember all that; let's call it something different." But Fall Out Boy flies in the face of this convention. They think their fans will get a kick out of the tricky names—and they seem to be right.

Beyond the titles, many fans—especially those who call themselves "emo kids"—enjoy the songs for the cleverness and the

Fall Out Boy poses for the Fuse TV show *The Sauce* in New York City.

emotionally open quality of the lyrics. They also like that the topics deal with everyday situations. Fall Out Boy's songs make a perfect soundtrack to the typical American teen's life, giving him or her something to relate to.

Song Structure

Fall Out Boy, like most bands, works within a simple song structure. They have verses, a chorus, and sometimes a bridge. Even if those musical terms don't mean much to you, if you're a music fan you probably know this form well—so well, you don't even notice it.

The verse is the part of the song in which the story is usually told. Each verse shares a tune or melody but has different lyrics.

Usually, each verse of the song moves the story a little further along. The verses are separated by a repeated piece of music called the chorus.

The chorus is often the first part of a song you can memorize easily—because you hear it so many times. It gets played in between every verse and sometimes gets doubled at the end of the song. That means you might hear a chorus four to six times every time the song plays. These little songs within songs are usually the catchiest part of the tune and contain the central idea of the song.

Fall Out Boy appreciates the magic of this form and generally sticks to the verse-chorus structure when it comes to songwriting. Occasionally, they throw in a sliver of music called a bridge between the verse and chorus, but for the most part it's a simple rotation. The repetitive and predictable aspects make the songs easy to sing or dance to. It's the kind of song our ears are comfortable with—and Fall Out Boy is happy to cater to our musical comfort.

Style

It's not song structure that has earned Fall Out Boy high praise in the world of pop. What gets them kudos (and fans) is the style in which they play. Popular music—music you hear on most radio stations—is broken into many, many categories. Fall Out Boy's music is called different things by different people; and all of them are right in some ways.

Punk

Punk rock is as much an attitude as it is a style of music. It began in the 1970s and 1980s as a rebellious, anti-establishment, countercultural style. It was the favorite musical style of the working-class youth of the time.

The Ramones, one of the first and most beloved punk bands, play the Palladium in Hollywood, California.

If you don't recognize it from the attitude, you might know it from the raging guitars and straight-ahead drum beats. To hear a true punk sound, listen to bands like the Sex Pistols or the Ramones. While they have different sounds—and accents—you'll hear some similarities in terms of speed, chords, and drumming style. Punk is simple. It's more about aggression and emotion than musical complexity. As you listen, compare the classic punk sound to Fall Out Boy's musical style. Do you hear any similarities? Any differences?

Pop

What keeps Fall Out Boy's sound from being classified as pure punk is the big dose of pop thrown into the mix. Where punk music rebels against the system, pop music is usually more conventional. A pop band's rebellion is in finding a new sound, bringing something unique to a familiar format. Great pop bands like the Beatles and the Rolling Stones redefined the music of their times. This is the dream of the pop band.

Fall Out Boy isn't as revolutionary as a band like the Beatles, but it does bring something new to the world of pop music: it's added a lot to the popularity of a musical style called emo, which is a great blend of punk and pop.

Hüsker Dü helped give rise to the emo sound—and ultimately to bands like Fall Out Boy.

Emo

In the beginning, the term referred to a new style of punk—one with more emotional range than the simple anger that punk tapped into. Short for "emotive" or "emotional hardcore," emo had a more ironic and melodramatic slant to it. Bands like Rites of Spring and Hüsker Dü are often referred to as the roots of the genre, but emo has come a long way since those bands.

TEENS AND DEPRESSION

Are you confused about whether your feelings are normal teen feelings or real depression? The National Mental Health Association (NMHA) offers help. According to the NMHA, "These symptoms may indicate depression, particularly when they last for more than two weeks":

- Poor performance in school
- Withdrawal from friends and activities
- Sadness and hopelessness; anger and rage
- Lack of enthusiasm, energy, or motivation
- Poor self-esteem or guilt
- Indecision, lack of concentration, or forgetfulness
- Changes in eating or sleeping patterns
- Substance abuse
- Problems with authority
- Suicidal thoughts or actions

The NMHA also offers these suggestions:

- Try to make new friends. Healthy relationships with peers are central to teens' self-esteem.
- Participate in sports, job, school activities, or hobbies. Staying busy helps teens focus on positive activities.
- Join organizations that offer programs for young people.
- Ask a trusted adult for help.

The style became so popular that it—like punk—branched out from being a descriptor used just for music. Today, emo refers as much to a look, attitude, and lifestyle as it does a specific musical style.

The Emo Lifestyle

Emo kids pride themselves on being very emotional. They may cry over sad lyrics or feel sulky and blue—or just act like they do. A certain amount of this is normal teen angst. Most teens, because they are growing and changing so quickly, feel sad or depressed. Some of that has to do with hormones and the normal processes of puberty.

Maybe emo is a way for kids to experience and share the normal moodiness of being a teen while enjoying some good music and fun fashion at the same time. If so, it's a healthy way to be comfortable with the moods and changes of being a teen. If, however, you can't seem to feel better and start to think of things like hurting yourself, then you've gone way beyond normal emo. You could be dealing with serious depression.

Depression is treatable. See a professional for help.

Chapter Three

Fall Out Boy, Album by Album

Fall Out Boy's music is very dramatic and vivid. A lot of the songs tell a story, almost the way a show tune might. While some have criticized Fall Out Boy for producing songs that all sound the same, on second listen one begins to know the characters and stories in the songs. And the dance beat? That's just icing on the cake!

Evening Out with Your Girlfriend

While this is Fall Out Boy's first release, it's not how most listeners got to know the band, as it was meant to be more of a "demo" or a rough sketch to familiarize record executives, disc jockeys, and other professionals with the group's sound. A reviewer for MP3.com described the album as "a Fall Out Boy primer, a

Fall Out Boy's first album was released in 2002 and was later reissued following the success of their subsequent albums.

hyper tantrum of humor, self-deprecation, puppy love, and Get Up Kids worship."

Fall Out Boy's sound is always young and energetic, but this first album is exceptionally so. There's something just slightly unhinged about it, as though the band hadn't quite learned to rein itself in yet. Another thing they weren't doing yet is letting Pete Wentz write the lyrics. The lyrics on this album were written almost entirely by Stump. While it is instantly recognizable as a Fall Out Boy album, the band's personality changed once Wentz took over lyrical duties.

Take This to Your Grave

Wentz brought his signature sharp wit to bear on Fall Out Boy's second album. "*Grave*'s margins are littered with impossibly clever turns of phrase," wrote Johnny Loftus for the All Music Guide

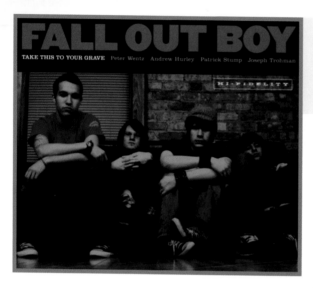

On *Take This to Your Grave*, Pete Wentz took over lyrical duties for the band. He remains the primary lyricist.

(www.allmusic.com). "A preliminary scan of the record's song titles is enough to prove this. From the double-time hardcore of 'Reinventing the Wheel to Run Myself Over' to the shifting dynamics of 'Homesick at Space Camp' (which was seemingly engineered by NASA to incite a crowd singalong), Fall Out Boy renders each song with a different mix of talents. Every time you think you've heard it all before, the band kills with another couplet."

While the clever lyrics are an important feature of *Take This to Your Grave*, the band also succeeds in creating a lot of great grooves. The chorus of "Dead on Arrival" is punchy, bouncy, and irresistibly catchy. The rhythm might make you want to hop on a trampoline, and it sounds like the song was made to be played at full volume. As for "Calm Before the Storm," there's no calm to be found anywhere in it. The drums are peppy, the vocals are vibrant and dynamic, and no matter what you're doing when you listen to it, you're likely to find yourself bouncing.

From Under the Cork Tree

From Under the Cork Tree is the album that introduced Fall Out Boy to the lion's share of its fan base. It's the release that sent the group to the top of the charts and on their way to stardom. It featured two top-ten hits in "Sugar We're Going Down" and the highly energetic "Dance, Dance."

Even though the characters in "Sugar We're Going Down" are indeed "going down," there's an underlying happiness and energy that threatens to bubble to the top. This is due largely to the song's danceable rhythm, a feature that is even more prominent in the

From Under the Cork Tree transformed Fall Out Boy from a suburban garage band to international superstars.

aptly titled "Dance, Dance." The video for "Dance, Dance" revolves around some awkward guys at their school homecoming dance, which has music provided by a live band. The members of Fall Out Boy play both the geeky guys and the cool guys in the band. The video is consistent with Fall Out Boy's oft-stated conviction that they are comfortable with being "geeks." They are capable of being both nerdy and cool at the same time, an ability that comes with being comfortable with themselves. The video assures listeners that they, unlike the characters in the video, won't ever have to feel uncomfortable at a dance where Fall Out Boy is playing.

Infinity on High

On *Infinity on High* (which sold more than 260,000 copies during its first week on shelves), Fall Out Boy seems to grow beyond its indie roots. Several songs on the album were produced by the well-know writer, producer, and performer Babyface; and the song "Car Crash Hearts" features a cameo by the hip-hop icon Jay-Z. Fall Out Boy is playing with bigger players, the stakes are higher, and the band seems to respond well to the pressure.

Yet, even as *Infinity on High*, with its high-profile guests and slick production, marks the band's arrival to the big time, the

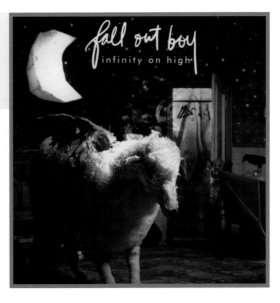

Infinity on High sold more than 260,000 copies in the first week of its release and featured contributions from Babyface and Jay-Z.

soul of the band endures. They're not who they once were, but they're not completely different either. "It's not an album," Rob Sheffield wrote for *Rolling Stone*, "of stylistic departures—in gems like "The Take Over, the Break's Over,' 'You're Crashing, But You're No Wave' and 'The Carpal Tunnel of Love,' these guys do all the things they're excellent at (mega-clever choruses, crescendo-stacking melodies, horrific puns) and none of the things they would suck at (saxophones, strings, slowing it down a little right about now)."

Chapter Four

Fall Out Boy Keeps Getting Cooler

So many people dream of being rock stars that it's hard to imagine that those who get their wish and attain rock star status might want something more. Well, it appears that some do—at least the guys in Fall Out Boy do. They're still busy learning, growing, and trying some very exciting new things.

Patrick Stump Tries Acting

Stump sings, of course, but he's not content to stop there. He's interested in pushing his artistic envelope by acting for television. The long-running NBC series *Law and Order* adds some spice to the shows by offering guest roles to celebrities of all stripes. In an episode called "Darkness," Stump played a "worker bee,"

Patrick Stump had a cameo role as a disgruntled office worker on the TV show *Law and Order*.

Patrick Stump on Law and Order

a young office worker who resents his wealthy boss and is upset about his lowly station in life.

"It was a real cool opportunity," he told MTV in an interview. "Anything you can take back to your band is. We go off and do our little fun things, but [Fall Out Boy] is always our main focus."

We can only assume his band mates had a great time watching him play a sneaky bad guy on TV. "It's cool," Trohman said in the same MTV interview. "They chose him because, well, look at him. Looking all sweet and looking all nice, but he's a real-deal creep underneath those glasses." It sounds like they'll have something to kid him about for quite some time.

Samuel Okumu is one of the child soldiers fighting at the Sudan-Congo border. Fall Out Boy has worked to raise awareness of this tragic situation.

Fall Out Boy Helps the Child Soldiers of Uganda

In recent years, many people have become aware of disturbing conditions in various parts of Africa and have wanted to help. The members of Fall Out Boy have taken an interest in this cause as well. It started, as many of Fall Out Boy's adventures do, with an idea of Wentz's.

Wentz learned of Invisible Children, an organization whose mission, according to its Web site, is to "improve the quality of life for war-affected children by providing access to quality education, enhanced learning environments, and innovative economic opportunities for their communities." In order to raise funds and awareness, Invisible Children created a fund-raiser called Displace Me. Americans could pay to be whisked away to a bare-bones camp. This was supposed to give them an idea of what life is like for kids who are taken from their homes to live in displacement camps.

Wentz signed up to participate in Displace Me. Describing his experience to VH1, he said, "I was at a very high point of my own narcissistic anxiety when I first started taking an interest in Africa . . . I'll be honest, I didn't really feel that moved. It was only missing the s'mores. That was what really made me decide that we had to go to Africa."

He and the band decided to go and check out the situation for themselves. They went to one of these displacement camps and filmed their video for "I'm Like a Lawyer with the Way I'm Always Trying to Get You Off (Me and You)." They hoped they could bring a little money to the area, do something fun for the people living in the camp, and raise awareness of the situation among music lovers in the rest of the world.

"We shot it on the cheap—we really spent most of the money getting to Africa and donating what was left to [charity]," Wentz told VH1. "The first time Patrick watched it, he cried. When I look at different images, they're upsetting for me. [In making this video] I was really proud of how far everyone in the band had gone, because each person had their own personal limits, and everyone surpassed them."

What did Wentz learn from the experience? He summed it up for *CosmoGIRL!* this way: "In Uganda, you get a sense that the kids are exactly like you, only they happened to be born in a different country and situation. Whatever you might imagine it's like in Africa, the displacement camps are even worse—they're extremely crowded and there's violence. At times we were actually scared for our lives. The things you care about there are very different; we couldn't pull up some Internet bio and expect someone to care who we were. The whole experience brought out something more human in us."

The Future of Fall Out Boy

Whether performing on network television or learning more about the lives of kids displaced by war in Uganda, the members of Fall Out Boy are busy learning, growing, and trying new things. They're not content to be merely rock stars. They're interested in seeing the world and learning as much as they can about their place in it.

Where will they go next? The only way to know for sure is to stay tuned. In the back of this book, we've listed some Web sites and other resources that will help you keep up on all the Fall Out Boy news. And there's sure to be plenty of it!

Timeline

January 2002 Fall Out Boy releases *Evening Out with Your Girlfriend*.

May 2003 Fall Out Boy releases *Take This to Your Grave*.

May 2005 Fall Out Boy releases *Under the Cork Tree*.

August 2005 The "Sugar, We're Going' Down" video wins an MTV2 Award; the song lands in the Top 40 charts.

January 2006 *From Under The Cork Tree* goes double platinum; single "Sugar, We're Going' Down" is certified triple platinum.

February 2006 Fall Out Boy is nominated for a Best New Artist Grammy; "Dance, Dance" goes double platinum.

August 2006 Fall Out Boy wins three Teen Choice Awards: Music Single, Track, and Rock Group; the "Dance, Dance" video wins a Viewer's Choice award at the MTV Video Music Awards.

November 2006 Fall Out Boy is the guest performer at the American Music Awards.

February 2007 The band releases *Infinity on High*, which sells more than 260,000 copies in its first week of release in the United States.

March 2007 *Rolling Stone* features Fall Out Boy on its cover; *Infinity on High* goes platinum.

July 2007 Fall Out Boy is featured on Al Gore's Live Earth concert lineup.

September 2007 Fall Out Boy wins an MTV Video Music Award for Best Group. "Thnks Fr Th Mmrs" is nominated for Monster Single of the Year.

October 2007 The single "This Ain't a Scene, It's an Arms Race" goes platinum.

Discography

2002 *Evening Out with Your Girlfriend*

2002 *Fall Out Boy/Project Rocket* (split EP)

2003 *Take This to Your Grave*

2004 *My Heart Will Always Be the B-Side to My Tongue* (EP)

2005 *From Under the Cork Tree*

2007 *Live* (EP)

2007 *Infinity on High*

Glossary

angst A feeling of anxiety, depression, and/or nervousness.

anti-establishment Going against authority and societal norms; rebellious.

bridge The section of a song written to connect the verse to the chorus or the chorus to a repeat of a chorus. Often includes key changes and modulations.

chorus The repeated section of a song.

extroverted A personality type that is energized by having lots of social interaction.

genre A style or category. Musical genres include rock and roll, country, punk, and jazz.

guyliner Eye makeup worn by a man.

melody A sequence of notes related to one another to form a musical idea. A song's main melody is often located in its chorus.

misnomer A name wrongly or unsuitably applied to a person or an object.

pyrotechnics Special effects involving fire or fireworks.

vegan A person who doesn't eat animal products of any kind.

verse The part of a song that consists of a repeated melody with varying lyrics. Verses are most often separated by the chorus.

For More Information

American Foundation for
  Suicide Prevention
120 Wall Street, 22nd Floor
New York, NY 10005
(212) 363-3500
Web site: http://www.afsp.org
According to its Web site, the
  AFSP is the leading not-
  for-profit organization
  exclusively dedicated to
  understanding and pre-
  venting suicide through
  research and education,
  and to reaching out to
  people with mood disorders
  and those impacted by
  suicide.

Canadian Academy of
  Recording Arts and Sciences
345 Adelaide Street West
2nd Floor
Toronto, ON M5V 1R5
Canada
(416) 485-3135
Web site: http://www.
  junoawards.ca
Canadian organization for the
  study and recognition of
  excellence in recording.

Web Sites

Due to the changing nature of
Internet links, Rosen Publishing
has developed an online list of
Web sites related to the subject
of this book. This site is
updated regularly. Please use
this link to access the list:

http://www.rosenlinks.com/
  cmtm/fabo

For Further Reading

Balling, Rich. *Revolution on Canvas, Volume 2: Poetry from the Indie Music Scene*. New York, NY: Grand Central Publishing, 2007.

Diehl, Matt. *My So-Called Punk: Green Day, Fall Out Boy, The Distillers, YellowCard—How Neopunk Stagedived into the Mainstream*. New York, NY: St. Martin's Press, 2007.

English, Tim. *Sounds Like Teen Spirit: Stolen Melodies, Ripped-Off Riffs, and the Secret History of Rock and Roll*. Lincoln, NE: iUniverse, 2007.

Greenwald, Andy. *Nothing Feels Good: Punk, Teenagers and Emo*. New York, NY: St. Martin's Press, 2003.

Saba, Jesse. *The Story of Fall Out Boy*. London, England: Omnibus Press, 2007.

Simon, Leslie. *Everybody Hurts: An Essential Guide to Emo Culture*. New York, NY: HarperCollins, 2007.

Bibliography

Greenwald, Andy. "It's a Holiday in Suburbia." *Spin*,
December 2005.

Kreps, Daniel. "Fall Out Boy, the Intellectuals? Wentz and Stump
Wax Philosophical on Gender, Tragedy." *Rolling Stone*,
December 3, 2007. Retrieved January 25, 2008 (http://
www.rollingstone.com/rockdaily/index.php/2007/12/03/
falloutboytheintellectualswentzandstumpwaxphilosophicalon-
gendertragedy).

Loftus, Johnny. "Review: *Evening Out with Your Girlfriend*."
MP3.com. Retrieved January 25, 2008 (http://www.mp3.com/
albums/2001 2008/reviews.html).

Montgomery, James. "Fall Out Boy Frontman Patrick Stump's
'Little Worker Bee' Won't Crack In 'Law & Order'." MTV.com.
December 20, 2007. Retrieved January 25, 2008 (http://www.
mtv.com/news/articles/1576817/20071219/fall_out_boy.jhtml).

Raftery, Brian. "On the Cover: Fall Out Boy." *Spin*, March 2007
(http://www.spin.com/features/magazine/2007/02/0703_
falloutboy).

StarWars.com. "The Rise of Fall Out Boy." October 27, 2005.
Retrieved January 25, 2008 (http://www.starwars.com/
episode-iii/release/publicity/news20051027.html).

Index

About the Author

Sarah Sawyer has a B.A. in vocal performance from Maryville College and years of vocal studio training. She is also an arts and lifestyle writer who has written for and about numerous bands and artists.

Photo Credits

Cover, pp. 1, 14 © Scott Gries/Getty Images; pp. 4–5 © Scott Gries/WireImage/Getty Images; p. 10 © Seth Browarnik/WireImage/Getty Images; p. 17 © Jamie McCarthy/WireImage/Getty Images; p. 19 © Jim Spellman/WireImage/Getty Images; p. 23 © Gary Gershoff/WireImage/Getty Images; p. 25 © Jeffrey Mayer/WireImage/Getty Images; p. 27 © Jim Steinfeldt/Michael Ochs Archive/Getty Images; p. 38 © AP Images.

Designer: Nelson Sá; Editor: Peter Herman
Photo Researcher: Amy Feinberg